Paley, Wearside

& Natural Theology

Glen Lyndon Dodds

Albion
Press

Albion Press
40 Park Parade Roker Sunderland Tyne & Wear
ISBN 0 9525122 7 0

First published 2003

For more information on other Albion Press titles
access http://members.tripod.co.uk/albionpress

Cover painting: William Paley by George Romney
By courtesy of the National Portrait Gallery, London

Typeset and Designed by UpStyle
www.upstyle.co.uk
Printed and bound in Great Britain

Contents

Preface

William Paley was a very prominent theologian and philosopher. Although his fame has diminished with the passage of time, he remains an interesting figure whose life and work are worthy of study, and was justifiably included in *The History Today* 'Who's Who in British History', published in 2000.

I have worked on *Paley, Wearside & Natural Theology* intermittently since the spring of 1995 and had hoped that it would be published in 2002 to mark the bicentenary of *Natural Theology's* publication. Unfortunately, for a variety of reasons that has not proved to be the case.

I wish to thank Liz Tinker and Ashley Sutherland of Sunderland City Library for obtaining necessary source material for me. Indeed, thanks to the conscientious work of the former, I was spared the task of travelling to the British Library in London to consult a particular work that proved hard to track down.

Glen Lyndon Dodds
Sunderland
18 December 2002

Prologue

The year was 1802 and an Anglican clergyman named William Paley was strolling around the grounds of his rectory. Everywhere he looked Dr Paley found something to enthral him: the plants, a butterfly fluttering past, or a bird singing from a nearby tree, all captivated him and strengthened his faith.

Suddenly, upon glancing at his watch, Paley – a most punctilious man who followed a set routine – realised that the time he had allotted to pottering around the grounds was over. He thus returned to the rectory and proceeded to his study.

There, quill pen in hand, he resumed a project upon which he had been engaged for a number of years. An accomplished writer, with several acclaimed works to his credit, he was nearing the completion of another major literary work – *Natural Theology* – which would become one of the most influential works of the 19th century and has been described as 'the standard exposition in English theology of the teleological argument for the existence of God.'[1]

Reference

1. *The New Encyclopaedia Britannic*a, vol. 9 (Micropaedia), 15th edition, (London, 1997), p. 84.

William Paley's Life Before 1795

A Brief Outline

William Paley was born in Peterborough in July 1743 and baptised in the cathedral the following month. He was the son of a clergyman and the grandson of a minor landowner of yeoman stock at Langcliffe in the parish of Giggleswick in the West Riding of Yorkshire, a parish in which Paleys had been present since the 13th century, if not earlier.

In 1745 Paley's father was appointed the headmaster of a grammar school at Giggleswick, an establishment that enjoyed a fine reputation among the grammar schools of northern England. Paley himself later attended the school. Reportedly, he 'soon surpassed his early class-fellows, by the exercise of greater abilities united to a more studious disposition than usually belongs to boys of that age' and 'was considered a very fair, though by no means an accomplished classical scholar.'[1] Paley's principal intellectual interest at this time was however mechanics, while his pastimes included attending cock-fights and angling: he had little aptitude for angling or sport in general for he 'was a bad horseman, and incapable of those exertions which required adroitness in the use of his hands or feet.'[2]

Paley, who was nicknamed 'Doctor' by his fellow pupils, attended the grammar school until he was 15. Thereafter, he received instruction in mathematics (a subject in which he proved gifted) from a young private tutor, William Howarth, at Dishforth near Ripon.

In October 1759 when aged 16, Paley entered Christ's College, Cambridge, at a younger age than was the norm – the usual age for entry into university was 18. He did not cut a dashing figure. His uncouth manners and dress caused amusement. Nevertheless he soon gained esteem through the power of his intellect and personality for he was a stimulating and amusing companion who reportedly frequently declared that 'A man who is not sometimes a fool, is always one.'[3]

Shortly after graduating in 1763, (he did so as Senior Wrangler, having achieved the highest honours in mathematics), Paley left Cambridge and gained a post as a classics assistant. The position was at the Greenwich Academy, a private school specialising in preparing boys for the Army and Navy. Here Paley taught Latin. Although fond of the language–for pleasure he read works by Virgil, Horace and Cicero throughout his life–he did not enjoy his spell at the school and resigned following a bitter disagreement with the headmaster.

During this period in his life Paley spent some of his spare time attending the theatre in London and was an admirer of the celebrated actor David Garrick, who was approaching the end of his stage career. Paley also visited the houses of parliament and the courts of law at London's Old Bailey. Coincidentally, he may also have heard reports that a young Austrian prodigy was in town, for Wolfgang Amadeus Mozart spent part of 1764–65 in London while engaged on a lengthy tour of Europe with his parents and sister.

On 23 February 1766, although a few months short of reaching the canonical age of 23, Paley was ordained to the curacy of Greenwich in Grosvenor Chapel, London, by Frederick Cornwallis, Bishop of Lichfield and Coventry. In his new post Paley was evidently fairly busy dealing with parochial duties. Moreover, he supplemented his income by acting as the tutor of a youth named John Ord. In June of the same year Paley was elected a Fellow of his former college at Cambridge. Nonetheless he remained at Greenwich for another year, instructing his pupil and attending to his duties as curate, after which he took up residence again at Cambridge, where in the course of time he held various administrative posts in Christ's.

Furthermore, from 1768 Paley served as an assistant tutor in the college and lectured on metaphysics, ethics and the Greek Testament. Subsequently, on 13 March 1771, he was appointed a tutor. As such, in addition to teaching the aforementioned subjects he proceeded to give a course of lectures on divinity. An impressive lecturer, he was able to hold the attention of his audience by his skilful use of illustrations and good sense of humour and did much to enhance the reputation of the college.

In 1771, moreover, Paley became one of the 'Whitehall Preachers.' Under a system established by George I in 1724, both Oxford and Cambridge provided clerics to preach in the royal chapel at Whitehall in the heart of London and thus Paley, who had been ordained a priest in the capital on 21 December 1767 (the vast majority of fellows at Cambridge were expected to be in clerical orders), periodically travelled to the city for his stint at Whitehall.

At Cambridge, Paley developed a close friendship with another lecturer, Dr John Law. This proved influential. Law's father, the Master of Peterhouse, Cambridge, was subsequently made Bishop of Carlisle and offered Paley a small rectorship at Great Musgrave in Westmorland. The offer was accepted and Paley was inducted to the living in May 1775. At this time, he met a young lady named Jane Hewitt (whose family was one of the most important in Carlisle) and they later married on 6 June of the following year. After his induction, Paley had returned to Cambridge, but in the summer of 1776 he resigned from his posts and journeyed north to begin life as a country clergyman. Although Great Musgrave was an attractive village, Paley preferred to live in nearby Appleby, a more populous and vibrant community.

That December, Paley received the vicarage of Dalston near Carlisle, but only began living there in 1780. In the interim, he resigned his post as Rector of Musgrave (he did so in September 1777) and, within days, was inducted to a more valuable living, the vicarage of St Lawrence, Appleby. His joint income from Dalston and Appleby was about £290 per annum, a comfortable but by no means great sum.

Further advancement followed. For instance, in 1780 Paley became a prebendary of Carlisle Cathedral and as such gained a prebendal house in the cathedral close. Henceforth, he appears to have resided in that city and in the vicarage at Dalston. He usually spent the summer months at the latter and, when resident in Carlisle, frequently rode to the parish. In 1782 Paley was appointed Archdeacon of Carlisle (the most exalted ecclesiastical position he ever attained) to which post the rectory of Great Salkeld was attached, although he does not appear to have resided there. It is sometimes said that his connection with Appleby now ceased but the episcopal registers show otherwise for he retained the living of Appleby until 1785. In the same year, moreover, Paley became chancellor of the diocese of Carlisle but nevertheless retained the archdeaconry.

It was in 1785 that Paley published a work entitled *Principles of Moral and Political Philosophy*. An instant success, it soon became a textbook at Cambridge where it remained in use until the mid 19th century, albeit subject to attack from various quarters by critics, some of whom believed that Paley's moral outlook did not give sufficient weight to the dictates of a Christian conscience.

Of the *Principles*, M.L. Clarke comments, 'in spite of a certain amount of traditional material his work has a strongly individual character. Its forceful style, telling illustrations, and sense of the realities of life distinguish it from other academic productions of the day…it has more life in it than some works of greater pretensions and greater repute.'[4]

As the book shows, Paley was essentially conservative in outlook and generally favoured maintaining the status quo. He held that one had a duty to obey the government unless a change for the better could be effected without disruption. Among other things, Paley did not believe that the vote should be granted to the mass of the population, whom he thought was unfit to play a role in determining the nation's affairs. He also favoured the retention of the death penalty for offences such as the stealing of sheep for he believed that it served as a deterrent; 'few actually suffer death', he wrote, (in most cases condemned individuals were not executed), 'whilst the dread and danger of it hang over the crimes of many.'[5] On the other hand, Paley was opposed to public executions. In addition, he argued in favour of religious toleration and voiced his disagreement with the slave trade. In subsequent years he remained committed to the abolition of slavery and, at Carlisle in February 1792, presided at a meeting held for the purpose of petitioning parliament to that effect.

By this date, Paley had been a widower for nearly a year – his marriage had produced ten children, of whom four sons and four daughters survived infancy. Furthermore, he had had his portrait painted. The second half of the 18th century witnessed the golden age of English portraiture. Those fortunate enough to afford the fees, could have their likenesses portrayed by celebrated artists such as Reynolds and Gainsborough, both of whom were based in London during Paley's days as a clergyman in the North West. They were rivalled in popularity by a younger artist from the north of England named George Romney. Born in Lancashire in 1734, Romney had been based in London since 1762, and in the years 1789–91 Paley ranked among Romney's numerous sitters.

In 1792 Paley was inducted to the living of Addingham, but evidently did not reside in the parish. The following year he gave up Dalston on being collated to the vicarage of Stanwix, which was only a short distance from his prebendal house.

During the 18th century some scholars, such as the Scot David Hume, wrote works in which they subjected the Bible to criticism: Hume, for example, censured belief in miracles and other aspects of Christian dogma. His views, and those of other sceptics, were of course familiar to Paley and moved him to write in defence of his faith and the authenticity of the Bible.

In 1794, for instance, Paley published one of his most celebrated books, *View of the Evidences of Christianity,* an exhaustive defence of the historical credibility of the New Testament. Characteristically an admirably clear work, it gained him a place in the first rank of theologians and the admiration of many fellow clergymen. At Cambridge, the book was to become required reading for undergraduates–no matter what their subject–and remained such until 1920.

In January 1795, as a result of the acclaim he had received as the author of *Evidences,* Paley was made Subdean of Lincoln by the bishop of that diocese. The post, which Paley held for the rest of his life, was worth around £700 per annum and required him to spend the first three months of each year at Lincoln. As events would prove, he would usually stay there until early May: 'It was to him a great delight to see Lincoln...in all its glory, and to view its numerous gardens and orchards in full bloom and blossom.'[6]

Directly after receiving the appointment, Paley made his way to Cambridge in order to obtain the degree of Doctor of Divinity. While there, he received a letter from Bishop Shute Barrington of Durham offering him the living of Bishopwearmouth which had become vacant owing to the death of its aristocratic incumbent, Dr Henry Egerton. Paley therefore vacated his posts in Cumbria (save for the archdeaconry of Carlisle, which he retained until 1804) and was inducted Rector of Bishopwearmouth on 14 March 1795 by the Rector of Sunderland, John Farrer, a clergyman with whom he was already acquainted.[7] Paley then returned to Cambridge to complete his degree, and arrived back at Bishopwearmouth later in the year.

Notes & References

1. G.W. Meadley, *Memoirs of William Paley,* (Sunderland, 1809), p. 3.
2. Ibid., p. 4.
3. Ibid., p. 10.
4. M.L. Clarke, *Paley: Evidences for the Man,* (London, 1974), p. 59.
5. *Principles,* p. 133, in *The Works of William Paley D.D., Complete in One Volume,* (Edinburgh, 1828), hereinafter referred to as *Complete Works.*
6. Edmund Paley (ed.) *An account of the Life and Writings of William Paley,* 1825, p. 316. (Reprinted Farnborough, Hants. by Gregg International Publishers, 1970). Hereinafter referred to as E.P.
7. Shortly after Paley's induction, Farrer resigned his post as Rector of Sunderland and was appointed to the vicarage of Stanwix by the Bishop of Carlisle so that he could be closer to his daughter who was resident in that city.

Paley & Wearside

As Rector of Bishopwearmouth, Paley held one of the richest livings in England (its annual income, derived from tithes and glebe, was approximately £1,200) and an estate, the Rectory Manor, comprising 240 acres. At the time of his induction Paley was still a widower, but in December 1795 he remarried. His bride was a middle-aged woman, Catherine Dobinson of Carlisle.

The parish of Bishopwearmouth, whose northern boundary was formed by the River Wear, was vast (it was nearly 20 square miles in extent) and at the time of the first national census in 1801 had a population of 7,806 people, most of whom, 6,126 souls, lived in Bishopwearmouth itself. Bishopwearmouth had once been the most important community in the vicinity but had been outshone by its burgeoning neighbour, Sunderland, about a mile to the east (part of the parish until 1719) and was indeed described as 'little better' than a suburb of its vibrant neighbour by a contemporary directory.[1]

Several roads converged on Bishopwearmouth. One such, along which Paley doubtless journeyed to his new living, was a turnpike road from Durham City. It approached the village from the south-west, flanked by fields. An evocative map drawn up in the 1780s by John Rain and known as the *Eye Plan*, portrays a tollgate a short distance from where the road reached Bishopwearmouth. Here anyone using the highway had to pay a fee for doing so. On the north side of the road, immediately after the tollgate, was a windmill. Shortly beyond this the road turned north and briefly skirted the south-west corner of Bishopwearmouth, before veering east and coming out near the heart of the village to link up with a thoroughfare on a north-south axis, today's Low Row and Green Terrace.

Directly to the east of this point, and on elevated ground beyond properties that included an almshouse founded in 1721 following the death of the Rector of Bishopwearmouth, John Bowes, (who had left money for such a purpose), lay the

15

modest village green. On the other hand, on a commanding
position a short distance to the north-east of the spot where
the road from Durham terminated, lay the parish church, St
Michael's, a somewhat decrepit old building that may have
contained late Saxon fabric and had undergone additions and
alterations over the years but was still essentially medieval at
this date–it has been almost entirely rebuilt since Paley's day
and is now known as Sunderland Minster. Francis Burgoyne,
who held the rectorship in the years 1595–1633, had installed
Jacobean pews and a new pulpit on which was carved the
date, 1632. The church could seat several hundred people and
dominated the community.

The historian, William Hutchinson, wrote a description of
St Michael's not long before Paley arrived on the scene. Among
other things, Hutchinson recorded that the nave had two aisles
'formed by two rows of three round columns…supporting
circular arches', and that the nave and its aisles were 'regularly
stalled with oak and carved with fleur de lys.' There was,
moreover, a gallery at the west end of the nave. Of the chancel,
he comments, *inter alia*, that 'on each side [it] is double stalled
with oak, in the cathedral form' and that it was entered from
the nave via a 'lofty pointed arch, rising from a cluster of
small round pilasters; closed with stalls and a handsome wood
screen, suitable to the rest of the chancel.'[2]

Just to the north of the church, and on the opposite side of
the main road running between Bishopwearmouth and Sunderland (the road is now High Street West), was the rectory.
Set back a short distance from the highway, the house had a
medieval core but had been substantially altered and extended
in the late 17th and early 18th centuries. One of the rectors
responsible for this was Dr John Smith, who became rector
in July 1704 and retained the living until 1715. He found
the building in a state of disrepair and so spent £600 on
the property, above whose main entrance he placed his coat
of arms. Hence to a large extent, and especially as far as the
principal facade was concerned, the rectory had a Queen Anne
character, though the interior retained some old features such
as thick walls, wall panelling and old wooden ceilings.

A document of 1792–a Glebe Terrier dealing with the
rector's property–states that the rectory was built of stone and
brick, had a blue slate roof, and contained 12 rooms. It was in

excellent condition, thanks to recent expenditure by Egerton, and moved Paley to comment when writing to a friend:

> ...such a house! I was told at Durham, that it is one of the best parsonages in England; and that there are not more than three bishops that have better. There is not a shilling to be laid out upon it, and you might have rubbed it from top to bottom with a white handkerchief without soiling it.[3]

In addition to the rectory were several ancillary structures such as a large barn, three stables for eleven horses, a cow house, and a coach house. Moreover, the *Eye Plan* depicts a small walled ornamental garden just to the north of the parsonage. The formal garden was adjoined by an enclosed area, 'the Park', which principally lay to the north, reached most of the way to the river, and was again part of the rector's estate. It was enclosed by a wall constructed by Egerton. Although industry had made its mark in the vicinity, the park nevertheless greatly enhanced the setting of the rectory and contributed to the status and quality of life enjoyed by the holders of the living. During his period as rector Paley frequently rode around the park on horseback for the benefit of his health. Of the grounds in general he said: 'There is nearly a mile I think of wall planted with fruit-trees; *i.e.* a rich field of ten acres, surrounded with a well-gravelled walk, garden and shrubbery grounds, commanding some pretty views of the banks of the Wear, two or three hot-houses and a green-house.'[4]

To the west of the park, and again part of the rector's property, was the Rector's Gill, a little valley through which a stream (described as 'the Burns' by Rain) flowed northward to join the Wear. Running along the north side of the park was a footpath. Many of those who made their way along it were workers en route to or from Deptford, an industrial suburb beside the river. Deptford lay a short distance to the north-west of the park and beyond some workers' cottages located at the mouth of the Rector's Gill. Glassmaking had occurred at Deptford since the late 17th century. Furthermore when Paley arrived on Wearside, a factory–that of Webster and Grimshaw–had just come into operation at Deptford and was producing the first machine-made rope in the world.

At home, Paley followed a fixed routine:

> Very soon after his first coming to Wearmouth, he began
> to arrange the employment of his time so, that when he
> was not necessarily absent from home every hour should
> have its employment…he acted in this most methodi-
> cally…in his garden he limited himself to one hour at a
> time, twice a day; in reading books of amusement, one
> hour at breakfast, and another in the evening; one for
> dinner and his newspaper….His public duties had their
> own time, as far as it was possible to accommodate cir-
> cumstances to such a method; at least they seldom made
> any alteration in his domestic life, as far as was apparent
> to those about him. His professional pursuits rarely inter-
> fered with the time devoted to his family, or to society;
> neither were these last suffered to interrupt his studies.[5]

Edmund Paley gives us a vivid description of his father
pottering around the rectory grounds:

> With the handle of his stick in his mouth, now moving in
> a short hurried step, now stopping at a butterfly, a flower,
> a snail, etc.; at one instant pausing to consider the subject
> of his next sermon, at the next carrying the whole weight
> and intent of his mind to the arranging some pots in his
> greenhouse, or preparing with the greatest gravity to
> remove some stick or stand that offended his eye, he
> presented the most prominent feature of his mind very
> obviously, but made it perhaps happy for his public
> character that he chose to be alone.[6]

Shortly after Paley became rector, some of the parish's leading
landowners approached him on the subject of tithes, which
could prove a source of friction between the holder of a parish
and his parishioners. Paley thus granted the six gentlemen in
question a lease for the length of his incumbency. The lessees
were to pay £700 per annum, even though the tithes' value
in the three preceding years had been £750. According to his
subsequent friend and biographer, George Wilson Meadley,
Paley 'found himself perfectly at ease by this arrangement,
and, when he heard of a bad crop, used to say – "Aye, aye, now,
I am well off; my tythes are safe, and I have nothing to do with
them, or to think about them."'[7] When, however, it is borne
in mind that this was a period of rising agricultural prices the

lessees evidently did well out of the arrangement. Nonetheless, as M.L. Clarke has written: 'The arrangement he [Paley] made at least ensured peace and relieved him of one of the vexations of clerical life.'[8]

In connection with his glebe lands, and particularly a limestone quarry, (the glebe mostly lay to the west of Bishop-wearmouth) Paley granted long leases on terms favourable to the tenants. This meant that he did not benefit when a great rise in the value of landed property ensued. As Meadley notes, Paley's 'tenants had very advantageous bargains: a circumstance to which he sometimes, indeed, alluded in conversation, but without the least marks of dissatisfaction or regret.'[9]

When William Paley arrived at Bishopwearmouth in 1795 a major engineering feat was nearing completion. This was the construction of the first Wearmouth Bridge, a short distance to the north east of the rectory grounds–the south side of the bridge lay in Bishopwearmouth parish. For generations the usual method of crossing the river had been by ferry. However, many inhabitants of Wearside had tired of crossing the river in such a manner. Doing so could prove time consuming and even dangerous, (in 1795, itself, at least 17 people perished when the Sunderland ferry capsized on 20 April while en route to Monkwearmouth Shore on the opposite bank). Hence they pressed for the provision of a bridge and in 1792 the necessary legislation was passed by parliament. Work on the structure began in 1793 and was completed in 1796.

A key figure in the bridge's construction was Thomas Wilson, a local schoolmaster with an aptitude for engineering who had been charged with supervising the project. Indeed, according to John James, most 'modern writers accord the design honours [for the bridge] to Wilson, who was undoubtedly the official architect/engineer, although it is probable that most of the ironwork details were due to the foundry experts at Rotherham.'[10] Paley became acquainted with Wilson and more than once was taken by him to the local workshops where equipment for the project was being produced, and where Paley examined the screws and pins with which the structure was being put together.

The bridge engendered great excitement, indeed wonderment. It was the largest single-arch cast iron bridge in the world and Paley showed it to visitors, a point noted by Meadley:

From the door of the park, which leads from the rectory house to the banks of the River Wear, Dr Paley could give his visitors a striking view of this elegant structure, with every advantage of surprise. He appears, indeed, to have been highly pleased with the prospect himself, and to have paid particular attention to the construction of the arch.[11]

Paley was present when the bridge was opened, amid much ceremony, on 9 August 1796 by HRH Prince William of Gloucester. At about 11am a long procession, consisting of several hundred freemasons and many other individuals, including local clergy and magistrates, set off from the centre of local freemasonry, Phoenix Lodge in Queen Street, Sunderland, a building erected in the mid 1780s and which still stands. The procession moved north and, upon reaching the junction of Queen Street and High Street (Sunderland's main thoroughfare) headed westward along the latter en route to the bridge whose southern end lay two hundred metres or so to the north of High Street. Upon reaching the centre of the bridge, an oration was delivered by the Reverend Nesfield, the Provincial Grand Chaplain. Subsequently, the procession returned to Sunderland and, after meeting in the parish church, moved to the nearby Assembly Room where a light meal was provided.

A convivial person, Paley frequently acted as host to guests at the rectory and did so 'in a handsome, but by no means ostentatious style.'[12] Meadley was one of those who benefited from Paley's hospitality, as was Paley's longtime friend, Dr John Law, now the Bishop of Elphin in Ireland. Another guest was a friend Paley had made during his days in Cumbria, J.D. Carlyle, the Professor of Arabic at Cambridge, who came to Bishopwearmouth in the autumn of 1801 and told Paley about travels and research he had recently conducted in the Levant.

Paley also enjoyed visiting his neighbours. 'He frequently mixed in card parties, and was considered a skilful player at whist; but he would, at all times, readily forego the game for conversation with an intelligent companion.'[13] Of his father, moreover, Edmund Paley noted: 'His wit, and talent, and pleasantry, made him a welcome guest any where….In a place of such mixed concerns as Sunderland, he had food enough for amusement and instruction, and he did not neglect it.'[14]

Among other things, Paley spent time talking to people

such as ropemakers, sailmakers and ship-carpenters, and plied them with various enquiries. Meadley relates that on one occasion they both watched a ship being launched, with Paley 'sedulously attending to the successive removal of the blocks by which the vessel was supported, and making enquiries of those who seemed most conversant in the business.'[15]

Shipbuilding was becoming an increasingly important facet of the local economy–in 1800 the Wear launched 12,662 tons, a figure surpassing that year's tonnage on the region's other main shipbuilding river, the Tyne. The shipyards were thus a significant source of employment. For example, one such, Laings', (founded on the north bank of the Wear at Monkwear-mouth Shore in 1793) employed an average of 72 workers in 1800. It should be noted however that shipbuilding was not the largest source of employment in the local economy. The exportation of coal was paramount and provided employment to numerous keelmen (who brought the coal downstream from mines inland) and sailors who transported it to destinations in Britain and elsewhere.

Sunderland's harbour also engaged Paley's attention: 'At the end of the pier, in a stormy day, he would be found conversing with sea-faring men upon their way of life, and acquainting himself with their feelings and sensations in a storm.'[16]

In fact, the harbour possessed more than one pier. The first such, the south pier, was erected in the 1720s by the River Wear Commission (a body set up by Act of Parliament in 1717 to enhance the state of the River Wear and improve the quality of the harbour) and had since been subject to rebuilding and realignment. Moreover, in the mid 1780s, the construction of a north pier had commenced and during Paley's days at Bish-opwearmouth work on the project continued. Furthermore, in 1801–2 the River Wear Commission's resident harbour engineer, Jonathan Pickernell (who had been appointed in August 1795) constructed an elegant 76ft high octagonal lighthouse at the end of the recently completed pier.

Paley must have watched as work on the north pier pro-gressed, and doubtless took a keen interest in the construction of the lighthouse. Given his interest in matters mechanical, he was presumably also keenly interested in a development that occurred within a few years of his coming to Wearside, namely the introduction of steam-powered dredging by the River Wear

Commission. In the summer of 1798 a 4hp steam engine began powering dredging equipment. Apparently, the venture did not prove successful for in 1804 the engine was sold and manually operated dredging recommenced. Nevertheless, Paley would have had an opportunity to witness the first attempt in history to use steam-powered dredging.

To reach Sunderland from his rectory, Paley no doubt usually made his way eastward along the principal road running between Bishopwearmouth and its larger neighbour, a road which as noted above ran right past his house and along which he must have travelled on numerous occasions. To the north, the land between the road and the River Wear was witnessing increasing development, whereas to the south it was mostly flanked by substantial houses with their own ornamental grounds. At a point occupied by Sans Street and Russell Street (both on a north-south axis) the road reached the boundary between the parishes of Bishopwearmouth and Sunderland and continued on, eastward, running the length of Sunderland where it was the main thoroughfare, High Street, today's High Street East.

As stated above, Sunderland exceeded the village of Bishopwearmouth in terms of population: in 1801 it had 12,412 inhabitants. When Paley became Rector of Bishopwearmouth, Britain was at war with Revolutionary France and had been so for two years. The conflict made its presence felt locally. For one thing, substantial wooden barracks were in the process of erection on a section of Sunderland's town moor a short distance from the harbour and seafront – they were completed in July 1795 and could house over 1,500 troops. Gun batteries were also present, although in this case they pre-dated current hostilities for they had been established to protect the harbour when Britain was at war earlier in the century.

At times, moreover, Wearside was subjected to the activities of press-gangs which seized 'recruits' for the Royal Navy, much of whose manpower was derived through impressment. Paley must have been well aware that during his days at Bishopwearmouth many local men, either of their own will or through compulsion, risked life and limb in the Navy, the best known of whom was of course Jack Crawford, who achieved national celebrity in 1797 for gallantry displayed at the Battle of Camperdown. On a more sombre note, the same year also witnessed a mutiny of the Channel Fleet at Spithead, and one of the delegates elected by the mutineers was likewise from Sunderland, namely James Melvin.

A number of French émigré clergy were given shelter in Britain during this period and some were lodged on Wearside in temporary barracks at Monkwearmouth, barracks that should not be confused with those mentioned above. Paley preached on their behalf and, according to his son,

> ...was particularly struck with the condition and deportment of many of them, with whom he was in the habit of conversing [as best as could be done through colloquial Latin] in his walks and near his garden.... He was glad... to offer them the use of his grounds, and his garden supplied many a cart-load of vegetables for their soup.[17]

For national defence, the British government not only relied on the Army and Navy but on volunteer units as well. A number of the latter existed on Wearside. One such was the Sunderland Volunteer Infantry, formed in August 1803. The *Newcastle Courant* of 27 August observed: 'They are to consist of ten companies of at least 60 men in each, and in a few days it is expected they will be completed. Upwards of 400 of them are already far advanced in discipline, and a Subscription has been opened for clothing them.' Later in the year, On 2 November, Colours were presented to the unit whose commander was Lieutenant-Colonel Sir Ralph Milbanke, Bt., of Seaham Hall. During the proceedings, states the *Newcastle Courant* of 5 November, 'an excellent Sermon was delivered [in St John's Chapel, Sunderland] by the Rev. George Stephenson, A.M., Chaplain to the Corps, in which he took occasion to pass a just eulogium on a late celebrated work of the learned Dr. Paley. After the Sermon the Colours were borne to the Altar Table [and] duly consecrated by the Chaplain.'

Who was the Reverend Stephenson? And what was his relationship to Paley, of whose *Natural Theology* he evidently made mention in the sermon? Born in Newcastle in 1759 and educated at Magdalen College, Oxford, Stephenson was a local clergyman–he had been appointed Egerton's curate in 1786 and retained the curacy until 1829. Hence Stephenson was curate of Bishopwearmouth throughout Paley's rectorship and was treated with great respect by him.

Something needs to be said of religion on Wearside during this period. Although the rectory and St Michael's Church were imposing, Anglicanism was not dominant in Bishopwearmouth. In part, as Geoffrey Milburn has commented, this was perhaps due to the wealth of the successive rectors, wealth 'which stamped [them] as belonging to the landed gentry, and detached them from a community which was increasingly commercial in its interests and activities.'[18]

Anglicanism was more vibrant in neighbouring Sunderland, where there were two Anglican places of worship in contrast to Bishopwearmouth's single church. Both were Georgian structures. One was the parish church, Holy Trinity, consecrated in 1719. The other, of which mention has already been made, was a daughter chapel, St John's, which had opened for worship in 1769.

The Church of England's oldest place of worship on Wearside, St Peter's, lay on the north side of the river (opposite Holy Trinity) in the growing community of Monkwearmouth Shore. The church was a historic structure whose earliest fabric dated from the late 7th century when St Peter's was built to serve as the main centre of worship for a monastic community founded by Benedict Biscop.

Interestingly, in the same year that Paley became Rector of Bishopwearmouth another clergyman with literary interests, John Hampson, became Rector of Sunderland. Formerly a Methodist travelling preacher, Hampson had previously served as Curate of St John's and as such, in 1791, (the year of John Wesley's death), had published the first major biography of the founder of the Methodist movement, whom Hampson had invited to preach at the chapel a few years earlier, an invitation that was accepted.[19]

Wesley visited Wearside on numerous occasions over the years – he first did so in 1743 – and of the nonconformist groups on Wearside such as Catholics, Baptists, and Quakers, the Methodists were foremost. Their principal meeting house in the neighbourhood was an elegant structure of recent date which lay on the corner of High Street and Sans Street and so was located on the east boundary of Bishopwearmouth parish.

Paley was not bigoted in his view of other denominations. It will be recalled that in *Principles of Moral Philosophy* (published in 1785) he had argued in favour of religious toleration – a view he had previously propounded at Cambridge, albeit in an anonymous pamphlet – and he remained broad-minded when Rector of Bishopwearmouth. 'His conduct as a clergyman was certainly formed upon a more true and enlarged principle of toleration than is often found, or at least than is often placed to the credit of the established clergy, in their intercourse with those of opposite sentiments.'[20] In the same vein, Meadley states that Paley was 'decidedly hostile to every species of intolerance and persecution.'[21] The same source continues:

> With the Methodists … who form the only numerous class of dissenters at Bishop-wearmouth, he carefully avoided every sort of altercation, and with a few of their leaders associated upon friendly terms. He also readily acceded to the application of Dr. Coke, one of their leading preachers, for a contribution to the missionary society, and civilly invited him to drink tea at the rectory.[22]

From Coke, incidentally, Paley heard about missionary work undertaken by Methodists in Ireland and among American Indians. A member of another denomination to whom Paley was friendly was an elderly Quaker gentleman whom he frequently invited to the rectory.

As rector, Paley of course preached in St Michael's Church. Meadley recalled: 'His accent was indeed provincial, his voice rough and inharmonious; but his manner was highly impressive, and his delivery marked by a peculiar force and energy of expression. Amongst those who prefer sense to sound, he was, at all times, a justly popular preacher.'[23] For his part, Edmund Paley noted that his father 'carried all his powers and all his heart into the pulpit … [and] showed himself free from any thing like affectation of solemnity or the pomp of priesthood.'[24] Edmund did not share Meadley's opinion of his father's voice and accent: 'His voice was not strikingly rough, but on the contrary in private sweet and very distinct…. Its roughness, if any, was on occasional exertion…. Neither was his accent peculiarly provincial. It might have been called rather wanting in refinement, but by no means disagreeably so.'[25]

A number of Charity Schools existed on Wearside. At this date (and indeed for years to come) some people of rank were wary of the idea of educating the children of the poor in case it gave them ideas above their station. Paley, however, gave encouragement to such establishments. One of the Charity

Schools existed in Bishopwearmouth itself and owed its existence to the generosity of a Quaker named Edward Walton who had made provision for its foundation in his will of 1768. The school provided a free education to a small number of Quaker children and other youngsters disadvantaged in some way.

Paley also supported local Sunday schooling and encouraged others to do likewise. Wearside's first Sunday School was established in 1786 primarily through the drive of a prosperous mercer and draper named Michael Longridge, a Wesleyan Methodist. As Geoffrey Milburn has commented: 'Longridge more than any other man was responsible for the launching of Sunday Schools in the Sunderland area...his was the moving spirit from the start.'[26] For a number of years the school flourished. But by Paley's day a decline had commenced. In 1802, though, a reorganization occurred. A body known as the Sunderland and Bishopwearmouth Sunday Schools (of which Longridge was the first president) breathed new life into local Sunday School provision and education.

According to M.L. Clarke, 'Sunderland was not a place which offered [Paley] much in the way of intellectual or cultivated society.'[27] The town, it is true, was no great centre of learning or social sophistication. Nevertheless, as has been seen, it was certainly not devoid of individuals who prized erudition and with whom Paley could enjoy intellectual stimulation. Longridge himself is a case in point for he was cultured and studious, and the same can be said of George Wilson Meadley. Indeed, both men were founder members of an institution which Paley joined soon after arriving on Wearside–the Sunderland Subscription Library–formed in early 1795 and of which Paley served as president for the second year of its existence. One of the volumes which comprised the library was Erasmus Darwin's recently published work, *Zoonomia*, in which some evolutionary sentiments were expressed.

From his youth onward Paley was keenly interested in the law–it will be recalled for instance that he had frequented the Old Bailey during his days in London–and as Rector of Bishopwearmouth he became a local magistrate at the request of the Bishop of Durham. As such, he is said to have been impatient and bad tempered. In his father's defence, Edmund Paley wrote as follows:

> His irascibility [as a magistrate]…was not at all unlikely
> to be attached to him in a place and neighbourhood
> where science and skill and penetration were confined
> very much to the trade and commerce of a sea-port, and
> where shrewdness of mind, and…largeness of intellect,
> was little exercised on general subjects. Here he undoubt-
> edly felt his superiority, and was allowed to bear a good
> deal of sway at the [local] weekly session…. 'Accusa-
> tions,' his biographer Meadley very well observes, 'are
> frequently preferred against men of clear and compre-
> hensive intellect, when engaged in the examination of
> petty causes, which the folly, ignorance, or knavery of
> the parties or their witnesses alone render difficult or
> complex.'[28]

On Wearside there was a large number of drinking places,
taverns and the like. Paley believed that their ubiquity led to
intemperance and lawlessness. Hence to address the problem,
he resorted to 'greater discrimination in granting licences'
than had been the case and 'once earnestly addressed the
bench of justices on the subject, at the quarter-sessions [held
four times a year in Durham City]; but, being feebly supported
by the other magistrates, and actually discountenanced by the
community, his efforts were ineffectual.'[29]

In 1800, while at Bishopwearmouth, Paley was attacked by
a 'violent *nephralgic* complaint, accompanied with a species of
melaena'.[30] It has been suggested that the attack was perhaps
caused by a stone in the ureter (the suggestion was made to
M.L. Clarke by Dr Frewen Moor) but some are of the opinion
that Paley had intestinal cancer. As a result of his poor health,
Paley was soon obligated to cease performing sermons. As
Meadley recalled, in December of that year Paley preached a
sermon on honesty in St Michael's to,

> …a numerous congregation, who little thought…that
> many of them should never hear him more. With the
> exception of an occasional discourse on the Christmas-
> day immediately ensuing, this sermon was the last which
> he delivered in that place. His cessation from this part of
> his professional duty occasioned among his parishioners
> a very general regret: but the necessity of that cessation
> was to all apparent, in the severe and painful illness,
> which embittered the latter years of his life.[31]

The following spring, for instance, when at Lincoln, Paley experienced a renewal of the complaint. In 1802, moreover, he was unable to undertake his annual residence at Lincoln on account of yet another bout of ill-health caused by the same malady. Of this period, Meadley comments that Paley occasionally invited him to pass an hour with him 'during some of his intervals of freedom from excruciating pain. His mind was still calm and vigorous, his vivacity unimpaired, and he conversed with his usual energy on various topics.'[32]

By May, 1802, Paley's health had sufficiently recovered for him to be able to journey to the spa town of Buxton in Derbyshire where his health was improved to some extent by spending time in the waters. Paley visited Buxton at the recommendation of one of the North East's senior medical men, Dr John Clark, who was likewise ill and who had thus begun visiting the spa town for the sake of his own health and both men spent time in each other's company while there.

After an absence of two months Paley returned to Bishopwearmouth and, shortly after doing so, completed *Natural Theology*, a work upon which he had evidently been engaged for several years and whose completion had been delayed by his bouts of bad health.[33] It was not the first time that Paley had written on the theme of natural religion for in the late 1770s, when based in the North West, he had composed and delivered a series of sermons entitled 'The Being of God Demonstrated in the Works of Creation.'

In *Natural Theology*, however, Paley dealt with the theme in a far more expansive manner. At the start of the book, in a dedicatory page to the Bishop of Durham, Shute Barrington, written at Bishopwearmouth in July 1802, Paley stated:

> ...a weak, and, of late, a painful state of health, deprived me of the power of discharging the duties of my station in a manner at all suitable, either to my sense of those duties, or to my most anxious wishes concerning them. My inability for the public functions of my profession...left me much at leisure. That leisure was not to be lost. It was only in my study that I could repair my deficiencies in the church; it was only through the press that I could speak.[34]

In October 1802 Paley's friend, the Bishop of Elphin – who had corresponded with him on the wonders of nature while Paley was writing *Natural Theology* – wrote to him as follows:

> I am reperusing your excellent work.... It will ... give a check to prevailing scepticism and atheism, and is cal-culated to do an infinite deal of good. It is exactly such a work as the world wanted; the arguments are propor-tioned to every understanding; many of the observations entirely new, and all treated in a new way, and expressed in your very best manner. [35]

In 1805 Paley journeyed to Lincoln, and at about the beginning of May duly arrived back at Bishopwearmouth. Soon after doing so his health collapsed. It never recovered. The end had come. 'He ... met the approach of death with firmness, comforted his afflicted family with the consolations of religion, and late on the evening of Saturday, May 25th 1805 ... tranquilly breathed his last.'[36] A number of incomplete papers were found on his study table at the time of his death. One, apparently the last work to engage his attention, was an unfinished sermon based on the text: 'Lead us not into Temptation.'

His body was transported to Carlisle and interred on 4 June beside that of his first wife in the cathedral. He left a substan-tial sum of money to his family and his widow soon returned to Carlisle.

In compliance with a codicil that Paley had added to his will, a posthumous volume containing a collection of 35 of his sermons was published in Sunderland by his executors and distributed free among the parishioners of Bishopwearmouth. Some of the sermons had been written before the onset of the illness that curtailed his preaching activity; others were written after that event with the intention of letting his parish-ioners benefit from their publication. The volume subsequently gained a much wider readership.

Of Paley, Meadley wrote that he was 'above the common size, and rather inclined to corpulence in his latter years.'[37] He also says that Paley 'was a good husband, an affectionate father, an indulgent master, and a faithful friend.'[38] In Meadley's opinion, in 'his latter days, he appeared to the greatest advantage at home; particularly when surrounded by an interesting fami-ly ... and by their young visitors, who frequently formed the happy inmates of his house.'[39]

According to Henry Digby Best, who knew Paley at Lincoln, Paley was 'a thick, short, square-built man, with a face which though animated and cheerful, could not but, at first sight, appear ugly; with bushy eyebrows, snub nose and projecting teeth; with an awkward gait and movement of the arms; a decent and dignified but by no means excessive protuberance of the belly; wearing a white wig.'[40]

Reportedly, Paley 'always expressed himself fully satisfied with his own lot, and showed himself satisfied by the great pleasure he took in reflecting upon his rise in life' and that in 'his study and his church he was ever intent upon the great object of his life, upon rendering himself useful in his station.'[41]

Candidness, affability and a sense of duty were some of Paley's characteristics, as were lack of ambition and a willingness to speak his mind and ruffle feathers when he deemed it necessary. He also had a down-to-earth manner and a keen sense of humour. Indeed, to Best, Paley appeared a common, vulgar, flippant fellow who never seemed to care seriously about anything and whose behaviour was thus at odds with his splendid literary reputation: 'I will tell you in what consists the *summum bonum* [highest good] of human life', Paley reportedly once said; 'it consists in reading Tristram Shandy, in blowing with a pair of bellows into your shoes in hot weather, and roasting potatoes under the grate in cold weather.'[42]

Paley also had a self-sacrificing spirit and could lead by example, as was demonstrated during a nationwide food shortage. His son Edmund recalled:

> In common with other parts of England, during the scarcity of 1799, resolutions were entered into by most of the opulent and respectable inhabitants of the county and city of Durham, to relieve the difficulties with which the poor and labouring classes seemed threatened, by stinting themselves in the use of bread corn, and their horses and cattle in the use of other grain. On a meeting being held in July of that year, for the purpose of devising means of lightening the general consumption, as well as providing soup and other substitutes for the poor, Dr. Paley drew up five or six resolutions...'to refrain from the use of puddings, pastry, and any sort of bread, except ordinary wheaten bread; to discontinue the giving of oats, beans, or peas to horses; to procure oatmeal, rye

> meal, beans, peas, and rice, to sell at a cheap rate; and to
> recommend to gentlemen to apply the leavings of their
> tables to soup shops, to be provided and supported by
> the townships and parishes.' This … was attended with at
> first indifferent success, though rigidly followed up in his
> own family and elsewhere …. Oatmeal, an article of food
> in many parts of England preferred before any other, was
> offered and refused; or when it was taken, was sometimes
> thrown on the ground before his gates; and he used to
> observe that during all that time of scarcity, when he
> was weighing out his own brown bread to his family, he
> had the mortification of seeing the poor people passing
> to and from the ovens in his parish with fine white cakes,
> dressed in all the pride of butter and currants.[43]

Of Paley's contribution to the world of scholarship, Clarke has
concluded, 'the reputation [Paley] once enjoyed was not wholly
undeserved. He brought to philosophy and theology valuable
qualities – common sense, clarity, humour, unpretentious-
ness.'[44] For his part, D.L. LeMahieu comments:

> … in both his theological and political works, he asked
> questions which often dig at the core of philosophy …
> [and] answered these questions with a thoroughness
> and lucidity rare in eighteenth-century divines. His
> statement of the teleological argument for the existence
> of God remains one of the clearest and most comprehen-
> sive in all philosophy. He is more consistent than Cicero,
> more thorough than Aquinas, more concise than any of
> his contemporary theologians …. No mere sidelight to
> the vast spectacle of eighteenth-century British thought,
> Paley was a dynamic transmitter of some of its most
> cherished assumptions.[45]

In 1895, a hundred years after Paley had become Rector of
Bishopwearmouth, a brass tablet was placed in St Michael's
Church to honour his memory. It was done at the request of a
fine scholar, the then Bishop of Durham, Brooke Foss Westcott.
The text, by Dr Vaughan, Dean of Llandaff, reads:

> In the closing years of the nineteenth century of which
> the first decade saw his death this memorial is placed in
> the Church of Bishopwearmouth to record the name of
> its most illustrious rector, WILLIAM PALEY, who after a
> youth of brilliant promise in the University of Cambridge

devoted his singular gifts of masculine thought and transparent language to the investigation of the principles of human duty, the elucidation of the witness of nature to nature's God and the confirmation by new and powerful arguments of the wavering faith of a doubting age.

Notes & References

1. *The Universal British Directory of 1793–98, vol. 4, part 1, N–S*, p. 515. (Reprinted King's Lynn, 1993).
2. W. Hutchinson, *The History and Antiquities of the County Palatine of Durham*, vol. II, (Newcastle, 1787), p. 513.
3. E.P., p. 272. The rectory was demolished in the mid 19th century.
4. Ibid., p. 272.
5. Ibid., pp. 289–90.
6. Ibid., p. 291.
7. Meadley, p. 127. G. W. Meadley was born at Sunderland in 1774 and made Paley's acquaintance shortly after Paley became Rector of Bishopwearmouth. Meadley was active in Sunderland's commercial, religious and literary circles. He also travelled widely. In 1796, for example, he sailed to the Levant and visited Naples, Smyrna and Constantinople whilst doing so. He died in 1818.
8. Clarke, *Evidences*, p. 47.
9. Meadley, p. 128.
10. J.G. James, 'The Old Cast Iron Bridge', in *Sunderland, River Town & People: A History from the 1780s to the Present Day*, eds. G. Milburn and S. Miller, (Sunderland, 1988), p. 9.
11. Meadley, pp. 129–30.
12. Ibid., p. 128.
13. Ibid., pp. 128–29.
14. E.P., p. 282.
15. Meadley, p. 183.
16. E.P., p. 283.
17. Ibid., p. 303.
18. G.E. Milburn, 'Religion & Society, 1780–1914', in *Sunderland, River Town & People*, p. 111.
19. G.E. Milburn, 'John Hampson's Life of John Wesley', *Sunderland's History 2000*, pp. 38–47.
20. E.P., p. 299.
21. Meadley, p. 163.
22. Ibid., p. 160.
23. Ibid., p. 166.
24. E.P., p. 103.
25. Ibid., pp. 105–106.
26. G.E. Milburn, 'Michael Longridge of Sunderland', in *Bulletin of the Wesley Historical Society, North East Branch*, no. 23 (Feb 1975), p. 25.
27. Clarke, *Evidences*, p. 49.
28. E.P., p. 307.
29. Meadley, p. 131.
30. Ibid., p. 135.

31. Ibid., pp. 167–168.
32. Ibid., p. 139.
33. According to J.R. Fenwick, 'Dr Clark often expressed his admiration at the fortitude with which [Paley] bore the most painful attacks, and at the readiness, and even cheerfulness, with which, on the first respite from pain, he resumed his literary labours.' J.R. Fenwick, *Sketch of the Professional Life of John Clark, M.D.,* (Newcastle, 1806), p. 27.
34. *Natural Theology,* p. 434, in *Complete Works.*
35. quoted in E.P., p. 335.
36. Meadley, pp. 155–56. Coincidentally, Paley's lifespan was the same as that of his exact contemporary, the gifted Italian composer Luigi Boccherini (1743–1805).
37. Ibid., p. 156.
38. Ibid., p. 180.
39. Ibid., p. 181.
40. H.D. Best, *Personal and Literary Memorials,* (London, 1829), p.160.
41. E.P., p. 16 and ibid., p. 292.
42. Best, *Personal and Literary Memorials,* p. 209.
43. E.P., pp. 309–11.
44. Clarke, *Evidences,* p. 134.
45. D.L. LeMahieu, *The Mind of William Paley: A Philosopher and His Age,* (London, 1976), pp IX–X.

Natural Theology

*N*atural Theology was published in 1802 and proved immediately successful. It was Paley's last major contribution to scholarship and its central premise – that God exists – was of course fundamental to his entire philosophic outlook. Previously, as noted above, Paley had written books on morals and the authenticity of the New Testament and he viewed *Natural Theology* (whose full title is *Natural Theology, or Evidences of the Existence and Attributes of the Deity collected from the appearances of Nature*) as forming part of a coherent system. In the book's preface, moreover, he admits that he had written the works comprising the system in the reverse order to which they should be read.

Paley begins *Natural Theology* with an analogy used by previous writers – such as the devout scientist Robert Boyle in the 17th century – and to which he frequently returns during the course of the book. No one, Paley states, who finds a watch would assume that it had made itself. It would inevitably be assumed that such a complex piece of equipment had a designer and a maker. Surely, then, the universe and life on earth betoken the existence of a grand designer, the supreme watchmaker? 'There cannot be design without a designer; contrivance, without a contriver; order, without choice; arrangement without anything capable of arranging, subserviency and relation to a purpose, without that which could intend a purpose.'[1]

Paley thus rejects the notion that the laws of nature could have come into existence without the agency of an intelligence: 'A law presupposes an agent; for it is only the mode, according to which an agent proceeds: it implies a power: for it is the order, according to which that power acts. Without this agent, without this power, which are both distinct from itself, the law does nothing, is nothing.'[2]

To furnish readers with compelling evidence of a designing hand, a master architect, Paley casts his net widely. Birds, plants, insects and fish, for instance, come under his gaze and are often described and analysed in great detail. Although not particularly interested in astronomy, Paley likewise inevitably says something about the universe. 'My opinion of Astronomy', he wrote, 'has always been that it is not the best medium through which to prove the agency of an intelligent Creator; but that, this being proved, it shows, beyond all other sciences, the magnificence of his operations.'[3]

One of nature's wonders that Paley cites as evidence of a Creator is the eye. Of the human eye, for example, he observed: 'In considering vision ... we can never reflect without wonder upon the smallness, yet correctness, of the picture.' He continues:

> Besides that conformity to optical principles which its internal constitution displays, and which alone amounts to a manifestation of intelligence having been exerted in the structure; besides this, which forms, no doubt, the leading character of the organ, there is to be seen, in everything belonging to it and about it, an extraordinary degree of care .... It is lodged in a strong, deep, bony socket, composed by the junction of seven different bones, hollowed out at their edges .... Within this socket it is embedded in fat, of all animal substances the best adapted both to its repose and motion. It is sheltered by the eye-brows; an arch of hair; which, like a thatched penthouse, prevents the sweat and moisture of the forehead from running down into it.
>
> But it is still better protected by its *lid*. Of the superficial parts of the animal frame, I know none which, in its office and structure, is more deserving of attention than the eyelid. It defends the eye; it wipes it; it closes it in sleep.[4]

In Chapter Five, Paley touches on evolution. Some people, he states,

> ... would persuade us to believe, that the eye, the animal to which it belongs, every other animal, every plant, indeed every organized body which we see, are only so many out of the possible varieties and combinations of being, which the lapse of infinite ages has brought into existence; that the present world is the relic of that variety; millions of other bodily forms and other

species have perished, being by the defect of their con-
stitution incapable of preservation, or of continuance
by generation.... The division of organized substances
into animals and vegetables, and the distribution and
sub-distribution of each into genera and species, which
distribution is not an arbitrary act of the mind, but
founded in the order which prevails in external nature,
appear to me to contradict the supposition of the present
world being the remains of an indefinite variety of exist-
ences; of a variety which rejects all plan.[5]

Paley continues the point thus:

To the marks of contrivance discoverable in animal
bodies, and to the argument deduced from them, in
proof of design, and of a designing Creator, this turn is
sometimes attempted to be given, namely, that the parts
were not intended for the use, but that the use arose out
of the parts. This... amounts to such another stretch of
assertion, as it would be to say, that all the implements
of the cabinet-maker's workshop... were substances
accidentally configurated, which he had picked up, and
converted to his use; that his adzes, saws, planes, and
gimlets, were not made... to hew, cut, smooth, shape out,
or bore wood with; but that, these things being made,
no matter with what design, or whether with any, the
cabinet-maker perceived that they were applicable to his
purpose, and turned them to account.... Is it possible to
believe that the eye was formed without any regard to
vision; that it was the animal itself which found out, that,
though formed with no such intention, it would serve to
see with; and that the use of the eye, as an organ of sight,
resulted from this discovery, and the animal's application
of it? The same question may be asked of the ear; the
same of all the senses.[6]

Paley also asks: 'What does chance ever do for us? In the
human body, for instance, chance, i.e. the operation of cause
without design, may produce a wen, a wart, a mole, a pimple,
but never an eye.' He continues; 'never was a watch, a telescope,
an organized body of any kind answering a valuable purpose
by a complicated mechanism, the effect of chance.'[7]

Paley firmly believed in the benevolence of God and
discusses why some living things were designed to prey on

others. In part, he reasoned that predators played a valuable role by reducing the suffering that would otherwise occur:

> A brute, in his wild and natural state, does everything for himself. When his strength, therefore, or his speed, or his limbs, or his senses fail him, he is delivered over, either to absolute famine, or to the protracted wretchedness of a life slowly wasted by the scarcity of food. Is it then to see the world filled with drooping, superannuated, half-starved, helpless, and unhelped animals, that you would alter the present system of pursuit and prey?[8]

Of *Natural Theology*, LeMahieu comments:

> ...[it] was a magnificently written work. Its argument began with the opening sentence and continued, uninterrupted, for almost four hundred pages.... [Paley] had an almost uncanny feel for the possible attacks of his critics and intercepted their objections before they overwhelmed his argument. His replies were sensitive and penetrating. It can be said without exaggeration that Paley's *Natural Theology* provides the most consistent and searching statement of the teleological argument in the English language. The failures of the book are those of the argument, not of Paley. It is, and deserves to be, a philosophic classic.[9]

Natural Theology shows that Paley possessed a wide-ranging grasp of scientific knowledge and was well versed in the writings of other natural theologians. One such was John Ray, who had written an influential and very popular work first published in 1691, namely, *The Wisdom of God Manifested in the Works of Creation*. Ray had been a member of the prestigious Royal Society and was acclaimed as the foremost naturalist of his day. Another author whose work Paley consulted was the famous anatomist William Cheselden, a close friend of Sir Isaac Newton. Indeed, Cheselden's *Anatomy of the Human Body* (published in 1713) was the source Paley cited the most. Moreover Paley derived information from a number of his friends, such as the First Astronomer Royal for Ireland, John Brinkley, whom he met via John Law.

Paley's *Natural Theology* proved a highly influential work and remained in print long after his death. One of its admirers was Adam Sedgwick, a prominent geologist at Cambridge and in his *Discourse on the Studies of the University,* published in 1833, he strongly recommended 'the habitual study of this delightful work.'[10]

Another admirer of Paley was Charles Darwin, who read *Natural Theology* during his days as an undergraduate at Cambridge University–he entered Paley's old college, Christ's, in 1828. Darwin studied the book thoroughly and was delighted by it. Although he retained his admiration for *Natural Theology,* in time, of course, he began to think along different lines and published *The Origin of Species* in 1859.

Among scientists who dissented from the arguments in favour of evolution expressed in *The Origin of Species* were Sedgwick , the renowned paleontologist Joachim Barrande, and the brilliant French chemist Louis Pasteur. But their views, and those of likeminded scientists, failed to stem the tide. Darwin prevailed and Paley was widely dismissed as a prominent advocate of old-fashioned and unscientific opinions, and the analogy of the watch and the watchmaker was rejected as crude and redundant.

Since the publication of *The Origin of Species*, scientific knowledge has increased considerably. Has the design argument, of which Paley was such a leading advocate, thus been consigned even more firmly into the realm of obsolescence? Or are there signs that the tide may have turned to some degree?

On this point a physicist named Dr Alan Hayward has stated, 'it seems that Paley's design argument really is a force to be reckoned with once again.'[11] He continues:

> ...the case for the existence of the Creator is stronger today than it has ever been. In every branch of science there is a growing body of evidence that the universe and its contents have been *designed*–that things just could not be the way they are as the result of chance. This evidence has so much weight that even some eminent scientists who are unbelievers have had the courage to face it, although they take refuge in the notion of a Creative Universe.[12]

It is certainly noteworthy that scientists frequently use the word 'design', or related terms, when referring to aspects of nature. For instance Phil Gates (a botanist at the University of Durham) has written as follows: 'Leaves are the power stations of plants, designed to capture sunlight's energy and use it to drive chemical reactions that turn water and carbon dioxide into the sugars that plants use for growth.'[13] Furthermore, Janine Benyus observes: 'The tendon in your forearm is a twisted bundle of cables, like the cables used in a suspension bridge. Each individual cable is itself a twisted bundle of thinner cables. Each of these thinner cables is itself a twisted bundle of molecules, which are, of course, twisted, helical bundles of atoms. Again and again a mathematical beauty unfolds' and the tendon's structure amounts to 'engineering brilliance.'[14]

Michael Denton, a scientist specializing in the field of molecular biology, has stated: 'Even the smallest of all living systems...bacterial cells, are exceedingly complex....Although the tiniest bacterial cells are incredibly small...each is in effect a veritable micro-miniturized factory containing thousands of exquisitely designed pieces of molecular machinery...far more complicated than any machine built by man.'[15] Moreover, Professor Michael Behe comments, 'many biochemical systems were...planned....Life on earth at its most fundamental level, in its most critical components, is the product of intelligent activity.'[16]

Nature provides countless examples of 'intelligent activity'. Certain types of orchid for example not only bear a representation of a female wasp on their flowers but also produce the same odour as a female wasp in mating condition. Hence male wasps, which have come into contact with pollen, respond by flying down to mate and in so doing pollinate the plant. Migration can also be cited. Of birds, *The New Encyclopaedia Britannica* states: 'A compass sense has been demonstrated in birds, which navigate by the position of the Sun, stars, and the Earth's magnetic field.'[17] Moreover, Otto von Frisch has commented as follows: 'One female swallow ringed in Scotland made the journey to Africa and back five times and nested each year on the same rafter within a few feet of the previous year's nest.'[18]

The universe, which contains billions of galaxies (some of which dwarf in scale our own Milky Way, which has at least 100 billion stars), also provides food for thought. For instance, the celebrated rocket scientist Dr Wernher von Braun, the designer of the V1 and V2 rockets and a key figure at NASA at the time of the Apollo missions, declared: 'The natural laws of the universe are so precise that we have no difficulty building a spaceship to fly to the moon and can time the flight with the precision of a fraction of a second. These laws must have been set by somebody.'[19] It was a view shared by another genius, the British physicist and mathematician Edward Arthur Milne – one of the foremost scientists of the 20th century – who concluded one of his publications as follows: 'The present essay...has nowhere mentioned God. The First Cause of the Universe is left for the reader to insert. But our picture is incomplete without Him.'[20] More recently a leading physicist, Professor Paul Davies, has commented: 'Through my scientific work, I have come to believe more and more strongly that the physical universe is put together with an ingenuity so astonishing that I cannot accept it merely as a brute fact. There must, it seems to me, be a deeper level of explanation.'[21] Furthermore, Hayward states: 'By combining the data from nuclear physics with those from astronomy, an astonishing conclusion has been reached. The universe is held together by a whole series of physical properties that happen to be "just right" for the job. The chances against these being a mere coincidence are many billions to one.'[22] Hence Professor David Block has written as follows: 'We live in a very finely tuned universe. Our universe is a home. Designed, I believe, by the hand of God.'[23]

While some scientists believe that the universe (which is billions of years old) is itself intelligent and thus effectively Paley's 'watchmaker', a small minority adhere to direct creation. Moreover, some scientists are 'theistic evolutionists' and hold that God used evolution to bring about the different forms of life on earth and directed the process from time to time. For his part, Albert Einstein declared many years ago that nature reveals 'an intelligence of such superiority that, compared with it, all the systematic thinking and acting of human beings is an utterly insignificant reflection.'[24]

It is interesting to speculate how Paley would view matters if he were alive today. Possibly he would be an agnostic or even an atheist. On the other hand, perhaps he would conclude that there is sufficient reason for adhering to a belief in creation or for at least espousing the views of theistic evolutionists. Certainly, the case for evolution – although in some respects verisimilitudinous–is not as clear-cut as is often maintained on television documentaries (and elsewhere) dealing with natural history.

The mutation of genes is a case in point. Mutations are held to be primarily responsible for the development of different life forms but many evolutionists admit that such a view is problematic. Carl Sagan, after commenting that 'mutations provide the raw material of evolution', declared that most mutations 'are harmful or lethal', a point also noted by Peo Koller: 'The greatest proportion of mutations are deleterious to the individual who carries the mutated gene. It was found in experiments that, for every successful or useful mutation, there are many thousands which are harmful.'[25] As a prominent evolutionist named Theodosius Dobzhansky commented: 'An accident, a random change, in any delicate mechanism can hardly be expected to improve it. Poking a stick into the machinery of one's watch … will seldom make it work better.'[26]

Moreover, the fossil record (which comprises many millions of fossils that have been catalogued and identified), does not rule the idea of creation out of court. True, it contains many gaps, but of these gaps an eminent evolutionist Francis Hitching acknowledges: 'The curious thing is that there is a consistency about the fossil gaps: *the fossils go missing in all the important places,*'[27] i.e., between the main divisions of animal life. Furthermore, Stephen M. Stanley says that 'the fossil record does not convincingly document a single transition from one species to another.'[28] Darwin himself acknowledged 'the abrupt manner in which whole groups of species suddenly appear in certain [rock] formations', a point noted more recently by Professor John N. Moore, who observed in 1970 that 'Groups of both plants and animals [such as whales, elephants and hares] *appear suddenly* in the fossil record … all are as distinct at their first appearance as they are now.'[29] Some scientists thus maintain that instead of occurring gradually evolution happens dramatically through sudden, drastic changes in genes. For his part, Alfred S. Romer has commented, 'the general picture could reasonably be said to be consistent with the idea of a special creation at the beginning of Cambrian times'; Carl Sagan has written that the 'fossil evidence could be consistent with the idea of a Great Designer'; and Hayward has declared that 'the fossil evidence for evolution … is really much weaker than the public have been led to believe.'[30]

Much more could be said. But it is fitting to conclude with the following by two distinguished scientists, Sir Fred Hoyle and Professor Chandra Wickramasinghe: 'William Paley, a figure of fun to the scientific world for more than a century...[is] still in the tournament with a chance of being the ultimate winner.'[31]

It is a point to ponder.

Notes & References

1. *Natural Theology,* p. 437, in *Complete Works.*
2. Ibid., p. 436.
3. Ibid., p. 517.
4. Ibid., p. 442.
5. Ibid., p. 449.
6. Ibid., pp. 449–450. Interestingly, Charles Darwin subsequently wrote as follows: 'To suppose that the eye with all its inimitable contrivances for adjusting the focus to different distances [etc.]...could have been formed by [evolution] seems, I freely confess, absurd in the highest degree.' *The Origin of Species,* 6th edition, (London, 1929), p. 136.
7. *Natural Theology* pp. 448–9, in *Complete Works.*
8. Ibid., p. 538.
9. LeMahieu, *The Mind of William Paley,* pp. 57–58.
10. Quoted by LeMahieu, p. 169.
11. A. Hayward, *Creation and Evolution: the Facts and the Fallacies,* (London, revised ed. 1994), p. 58.
12. Ibid., p. 65.
13. Phil Gates, 'Leaves You Can Live With', *The Northumbrian,* issue no. 53, December 1999/January 2000, p. 44.
14. J.M. Benyus, *Biomimicry–Innovation Inspired by Nature,* (New York, 1997), p. 1.
15. M. Denton, *Evolution: a Theory in Crisis,* (Bethesda, 1986), p. 250.
16. M. Behe, *Darwin's Black Box: the Biochemical Challenge to Evolution,* (New York, 1996), p. 193.
17. *The New Encyclopaedia Britannica,* vol. 8 (Micropaedia) 15th edition, (London, 1997), p. 119.
18. Otto von Frisch, *Animal Migration,* (London, 1969), p. 63.
19. Quoted in (anon.) *Life–How did it Get Here? By Evolution or by Creation?,* (New York, 1985), p. 124. (The reference given is *National Enquirer* 10 Feb., 1976).
20. E.A. Milne, *Kinematic Relativity,* (Oxford, 1948), p. 233.
21. P. Davies, *The Mind of God–Science and the Search for Ultimate Meaning,* (London, 1992), p. 16.
22. Hayward, *Creation & Evolution,* p. 201.
23. D. Block, *Star Watch,* (Colorado Springs, 1988), p. 149.
24. A. Einstein, *Ideas and Opinions,* (New York, 1934), p. 40.
25. C. Sagan, *Cosmos,* (New York, 1980), p. 27 and p. 31; Peo Koller, quoted in (anon.) *Life–How did it Get Here? By Evolution or by Creation?,* pp. 100–101, where the source is given as *Chromosomes and Genes,* 1971, p. 127.

26. Theodosius Dobzhansky, *Heredity and the Nature of Man*, (New York, 1964), p. 126.
27. F. Hitching, *The Neck of the Giraffe*, (London, 1982), p. 19.
28. S. Stanley, *The New Evolutionary Timetable*, (London, 1981), p. 95.
29. Darwin, *The Origin of Species*, p. 268. The comment by J.N. Moore is quoted in (anon.) *Life–How Did It Get Here? By Evolution or by Creation?*, pp. 65–66, and the source given is J.N. Moore *Should Evolution be Taught?*, 1970, pp 14, 24).
30. A.S. Romer, 'Darwin and the Fossil Record', *Natural History*, October 1959, p. 467; C. Sagan *Cosmos*, p. 29; A. Hayward, *Creation and Evolution*, p. 42.
31. F. Hoyle & N.C. Wickramasinghe, *Evolution from Space*, (London, 1981), p. 96.